ECO ACTION

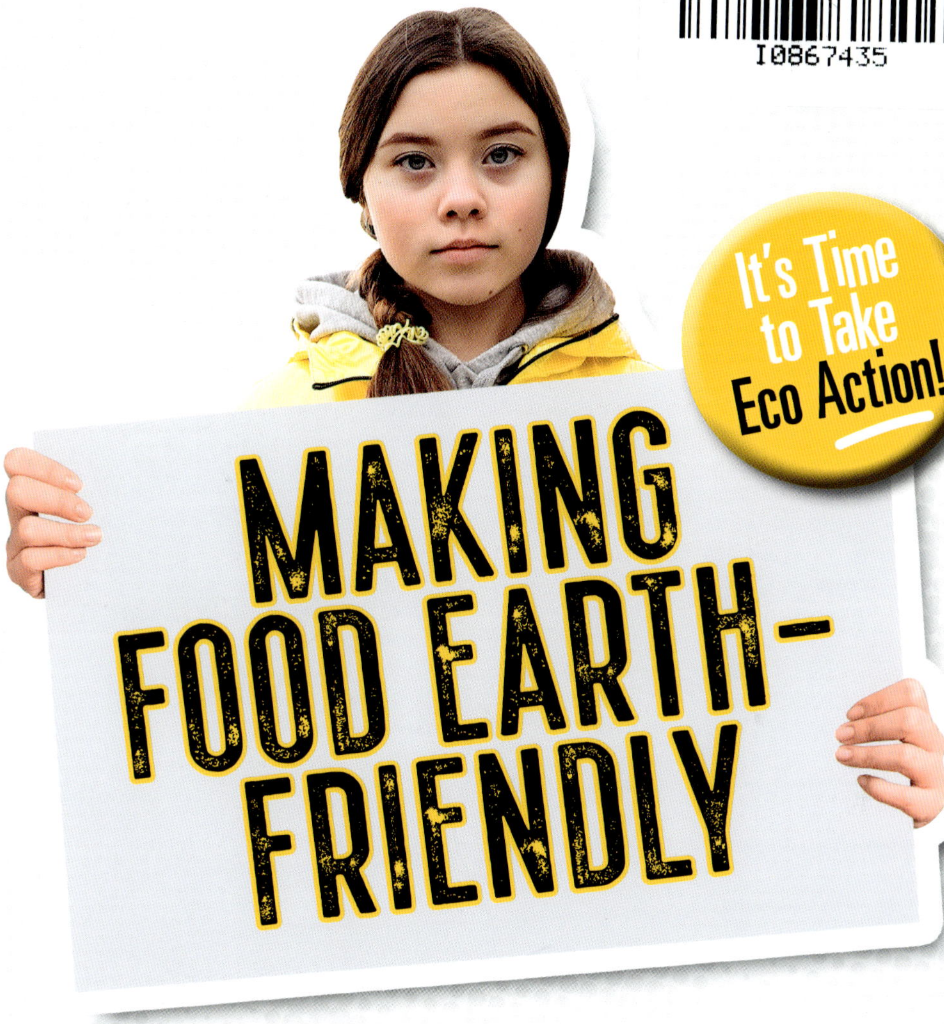

It's Time to Take Eco Action!

SARAH EASON

CHERITON
CHILDREN'S BOOKS

Published in 2023 by **Cheriton Children's Books**
PO Box 7258, Bridgnorth, Shropshire, WV16 9ET, UK

First Edition

Author: Sarah Eason
Designer: Paul Myerscough
Editor: Jane Brooke
Proofreader: Wendy Scavuzzo
Consultant: David Hawksett, BSc

Picture credits: Cover: Top: Shutterstock/Tim Roberts Photography; Center: Shutterstock/iVazoUSky; Bottom: Shutterstock/Arina P Habich. Inside: p1: Shutterstock/iVazoUSky; p4-5: Shutterstock/Ground Picture; p6: Shutterstock/Huguette Roe; p7: Shutterstock/Toa55; p8: Shutterstock/Pixel-Shot; p9: Shutterstock/Photographee.eu; p10: Shutterstock/Ringo Chiu; p11: Shutterstock/Ringo Chiu; p13: Shutterstock/Z.H.Chen; p14: Shutterstock/Joshua Aucoin; p15: Shutterstock/Mohamed Abdulraheem; pp16-17: Shutterstock/Rich Carey; p17: Shutterstock/Tunatura; p18: Shutterstock/Vicuschka; p19: Shutterstock/Chanintorn.V; p21: Shutterstock/Shane Myers Photography; p22: Shutterstock/Ammit Jack; p23: Shutterstock/William Edge; p24: Shutterstock/Slowmotiongli; p25: Shutterstock/Feathercollector; p26: Shutterstock/Tim Roberts Photography; p27: Shutterstock/Oneinchpunch; p28: Shutterstock/Jason Mintzer; p29: Shutterstock/PongMoji; p30: Shutterstock/Vladimir Lazarev; p31: Shutterstock/Arina P Habich; p33: Shutterstock/Rusana Krasteva; p34: Shutterstock/Lauraslens; p35: Shutterstock/Sundry Photography; p36: Shutterstock/Mr. Mixers Stock; p37: Shutterstock/Hari Mahidhar; p38t: Shutterstock/Jane Rix; p38b: Shutterstock; p39: Shutterstock/Kwame Amo; p41: Shutterstock/Don Mammoser; p42: Shutterstock/Juice Flair; p43: Shutterstock/Firn; p44: Shutterstock/Ground Picture; p45: Shutterstock/Nicole Helgason; Throughout: Shutterstock/Voy Ager.

Printed in China

CONTENTS

WHY WE NEED TO TAKE ECO ACTION

Food—we all need it! Food contains calories that we need for energy. Calories are units of energy. Food also contains **minerals** and vitamins that we need to stay healthy. Healthy food is good for us, but how we produce it and what we do with it isn't always good for the planet.

We can all help the planet by choosing to buy food that is created and packaged in ways that are not harmful.

The Problem with Food

Today, food is presenting our planet with many problems. Often, the way we create food is not sustainable. That means it is created in a way that is harmful to Earth and cannot be maintained. Our farming methods can be destructive, from over-farming the soil to cutting down precious forests to make way for farmland. Some forms of farming also use a huge amount of water. This is an important natural **resource** that we cannot afford to overuse or waste. And it's not just how we source food on land that is the issue. We have also harmed the oceans through overfishing.

A Package of Problems

The way that we package our food is an issue, too. Much of our food is wrapped up in plastic and other problematic packaging. That packaging is made in factories, which use electricity created by burning **fossil fuels** in power stations. That creates **pollution**, which harms the planet. We also transport food from far away, on planes and ships. They pump out pollution as they travel. That further harms the planet.

Landing in Landfills

And once our packaged food reaches us, what we do with the packaging is a problem. When we throw it away, it often makes its way into landfills. These are pits into which our garbage is thrown. And we waste food, too! The food that we do not eat is thrown into the garbage. That wasted food then also makes its way into landfills. Garbage such as food and plastic waste causes real problems in landfills.

It's Time to Take Eco Action!

So, what can we do to stop our problems with food? We can take action—eco action! Eco action is activity that helps protect the planet. In this book, you'll discover what actions people are taking to tackle our food problems. You'll also discover what actions you can take to combat our harmful food activities. And you'll also discover how you can build a green career that will help protect Earth for future generations. Are you ready to take eco action? Then read on!

CHAPTER 1

WHAT A WASTE!

Have you ever filled your plate with food only to eat half of it? Perhaps you didn't eat it all because you weren't as hungry as you thought. Or you didn't have time to finish the meal. But what happened to that leftover food? Did it end up in the trash?

Not Your Problem?

We have all been guilty of throwing away food. It's easy to scrape half-eaten meals into the trash. It takes just a second to toss an apple core. It's easy not to think about what happens to the food we throw away. After all, why should food trash be your problem?

It's the Pits

When we throw food waste into our household garbage, it goes on a really rotten journey. First, it is picked up by trash collectors. Then, it is taken to landfills. These are pits in which waste is dumped. In these pits, food waste is packed close to other waste, with little air in between. In fact, landfills have virtually airless conditions. So what's the problem with that?

In landfills, food waste is dumped alongside a lot of other waste. That includes plastic bags and cardboard waste.

A Gassy Problem

In a natural **environment,** food biodegrades. That means it rots, or breaks down. The oxygen in the air allows this natural breakdown. Landfills are not natural environments, and contain hardly any oxygen. Without a supply of oxygen, food in landfills breaks down very slowly. And as it does so, it releases a gas called methane. If that gas is not contained, it can be very harmful. When it escapes into the air, methane gas traps heat around Earth.

Like a Greenhouse

Methane is a greenhouse gas. Greenhouse gases are given off by human activity, such as dumping waste in landfills. They encircle Earth like a blanket. That causes the planet to heat up. Earth is getting hotter and hotter. That is causing **climate** patterns to change. Climate change is one of the major threats facing Earth.

Extreme weather events such as **wildfires** are damaging people's properties and businesses. They are also harming the land on which we grow our food.

CLIMATE CHANGE– WHAT'S GOING ON?

Climate change has always happened on Earth. It is the change in climate and the weather patterns the planet experiences. However, today climate change is accelerating, or speeding up. That is due to human activities. They include releasing harmful gases into Earth's **atmosphere** by burning fossil fuels and dumping waste into landfills.

Today, we are seeing extreme weather in many parts of the world as a result of climate change. That weather includes **floods** and **droughts**. It also includes **hurricanes** and wildfires.

FEEDING THE PROBLEM

Did you know that every year around 1.4 billion tons (1.3 billion mt) of the food produced around the world is thrown away? So, why does so much of our food go to waste? There are a number of reasons why people waste food.

Busy Lifestyles

Today, many people are very busy. People are often holding down jobs and raising a family at the same time. They may not have as much time to plan what they will cook and eat as they did in the past. That means people rush to buy food, and perhaps buy more than they need. They may then leave food in the fridge, uneaten. The food goes bad, and is then thrown out. People may also load their plates with more food than they need, then leave half of it uneaten. That food then goes in the trash, adding to food waste.

We are wasting vital resources by throwing away our food. It takes a lot of water, land, and labor to produce food. When we waste food, we waste all of those resources.

A HUNGRY WORLD

Food waste is a problem, but so is a lack of food for many people around the world. Every year, more than 821 million people go hungry every day. It's shocking to think that there is enough food on Earth to feed everyone on the planet. In fact, there is actually 1.5 times enough food to feed everyone on Earth. Imagine what a different place the world would be if we stopped our food waste.

In the United States alone, 40 million tons (36.2 million mt) of food is thrown away every year. Yet, one in seven people in the country are going hungry.

Too Ugly to Eat

Food is also thrown away by businesses that sell food. They reject it because it is seen as too "ugly" to be sold. People have gotten used to buying perfect-looking apples. They like their carrots to be perfectly formed, not wonky! They don't want to buy potatoes that look like they have two heads! We have become fussy eaters, and our food stores feed that fuss. They reject fruits and vegetables that are not perfectly formed, because they think people won't buy them. Those foods are then thrown away.

Stores, restaurants, and cafés even throw away food that customers would be happy to buy. If the food is not sold by the end of a business day, it may be thrown in the trash. It's a huge waste of perfectly good food.

TAKING ECO ACTION:

FEEDING AMERICA

One organization that is taking action against food waste is Feeding America. This awesome group was set up 40 years ago to help tackle the issue of food shortage among Americans. As the problem of food waste has grown in recent years, Feeding America is now also helping reduce wasted food by picking up that food and **redistributing** it among the people who need it the most.

Rescuing Food

In 2020, Feeding America rescued 4 billion pounds (1.8 billion kg) of groceries that would otherwise have been thrown away. That food would likely have ended up in landfills were it not for Feeding America. The organization collected the food from food **manufacturers**. It got food from food stores and farmers who would otherwise have thrown it away. The rescued food was transported to food banks. There, it was given to people who desperately needed it.

The Covid-19 **pandemic** has shone a light on the issue of **food poverty**. We need to make sure everyone has food, and that food waste becomes a thing of the past.

Smart Connection

Feeding America is now working on an innovative new program called MealConnect. The program links businesses involved with food. They connect restaurants, grocery stores, and hotels with local food banks. When the businesses have unused food available, they contact the food banks directly. The food can then be picked up from the food businesses, and taken immediately to the food banks. There, it is handed out to hungry people.

MealConnect is a win-win for people and for the planet. People who would otherwise go hungry are provided with meals. The food is transported locally, thereby cutting down on transportation pollution. And the food is not wasted or dumped in a landfill.

A HUNGER PANDEMIC

The Covid-19 pandemic has brought the huge issue of hunger to our attention. In 2020, more than 60 million people visited food banks in the United States. Many of them had lost their jobs and income as a result of the pandemic. Most of those people would have gone hungry were it not for programs such as Feeding America.

TAKE ECO ACTION AGAINST WASTE

Organizations like Feeding America are taking positive action against food waste. And there are positive actions that you can take to cut back on your food waste, too. By taking eco action, you will not only be helping the planet, you will be helping people in need, too.

Think About It

Before you load up your plate with food, think about how much of it you need or want to eat. Try to put only what you think you will eat on your plate.

Get Everyone Involved

Ask your school if it can help stop food waste. Check if you can get involved in food redistribution programs. Make your friends and family aware of the issue, and see how you can all stop food waste.

Make a Composter

We will always have some food waste, whether that is vegetable peels or an apple core. The good news is we can turn that waste into something useful, and keep it out of landfills. How? By making a composter!

How to Make a Composter

To make an outdoor composter, you need a large outdoor container. Use these actions to feed it:

- Start by putting a layer of soil in the bottom of the container. Then, put your food waste into your composter. That can include fruit and vegetable peelings. Eggshells, bread crusts, and any uneaten vegetables from meals can be included, too.
- Make sure that you don't include dairy products, such as cheese and yogurt. Meat, bones, fish, fats, and oils should also be excluded.
- Every time you add a layer of food waste, make sure that you add a layer of soil on top. It helps to stir the compost mixture every now and again too. Keep adding your food waste to the composter, and watch what happens! Over time, the waste will break down into a crumbly mixture that looks like soil. That is called compost.
- Your compost can be used in a garden to grow some of your own food, such as fruits and vegetables. That's a great eco action to take!

Eco Action Wins

By making a composter, you'll be sending less waste to landfills. And that means less climate change. If you have an outdoor composter, you may find that worms, creepy crawlies, and other creatures have made a home in it, too. In fact, you may have created an entire **ecosystem**! By getting involved with food redistribution, you'll help stop food waste and help hungry people—all big wins for planet Earth!

CHAPTER 2

PROBLEMS PACKAGED UP

How we package our food today is a problem. Years ago, most food came unpackaged. When people shopped, they put the food they bought in **reusable** baskets or bags. They were made of natural materials. Cheese, meat, and fish were wrapped in cloth or paper, not plastic. People often grew their own fruits and vegetables, too. Today, all that has changed.

Plastic thrown on the ground can blow away. If it lands in a natural **habitat**, it harms the plants and animals that live there.

Packed in Plastic

Now when we shop for food, much of what we buy is wrapped in plastic. We buy fruits and vegetables in plastic bags. We buy meat, fish, and cheese that have been wrapped in plastic. We buy yogurt in plastic containers. Our drinks come in plastic bottles, and some are packaged with plastic straws. In fact, it is difficult to think of food we buy that isn't wrapped in plastic!

Plastic vs the Planet

Plastic is a real problem for our planet. Plastic is not biodegradable, or able to be broken down by the action of living things. Unlike traditional food packaging such as paper, plastic does not rot when it is thrown away. Instead, it hangs around in the environment for years and years—hundreds of years, in fact. Depending on the type of plastic, it can take up to 1,000 years to break down. And when it does finally break down, plastic can leak harmful substances into the environment.

Plastic thrown in the trash often ends up in landfills. There it is a hidden problem. The plastic piles up—into a big problem that future generations will have to deal with.

RECYCLING—A MIXED PICTURE

We can all help reduce plastic waste by **recycling** as much as possible. Some plastic packaging is made from a strong, lightweight plastic called polyethylene terephthalate. It is better known as PET. Most plastic water or soft-drink bottles, as well as some food packaging, are made from PET. The good news is that PET is 100 percent recyclable!

Other food packaging is more difficult to recycle. Many forms of plastic cannot be recycled. Some food packaging is made from mixed materials. That makes it difficult to recycle. It might contain both metal and plastic, joined together in a way that makes it impossible for recyclers to separate. For example, potato chip bags can be made of both plastic and metal. Mixed material food packaging usually ends up in landfills.

PLASTIC IN THE OCEANS

Thrown-away plastic makes its way into habitats such as rivers and oceans. There, animals may try to eat the plastic. They also become caught up in it. Every year, 100,000 ocean mammals are killed by plastic in the oceans.

Plastic Danger

The biggest cause of harm to wildlife due to plastic is injury. Ocean animals become entangled in plastic waste such as bags, food wrapping, and plastic six-pack rings. Much of this plastic packaging has sharp edges, which can cut into animals. That causes severe injuries. Plastic can also prevent the animals from moving. For example, if a seabird becomes tangled up in plastic, it may not be able to move its wings. Ocean mammals, such as dolphins, need to come to the water's surface to breathe. If they are caught in plastic and cannot move, they will drown.

FULL OF PLASTIC

Shearwaters are birds that live along coastlines in many parts of the world. They are found in parts of the eastern coast of the United States. These birds eat more plastic than any other animal that lives in oceans or along their shores. The birds fill their stomachs with plastic. Plastic cannot be digested. That leaves them so full they do not hunt for food. As a result, they starve to death. Shearwaters also feed plastic to their babies. The young then do not get the nutrition, or goodness from food, they need. They may die, or be too weak to hunt for food when it is time to leave the nest.

Around 1,000 turtles die every year as a result of eating plastic bags.

Plastic on the Menu

Another problem with plastic in our oceans is that sea animals may mistake it for food, and eat it. Inside the animals' stomachs, the plastic cannot be broken down. It builds up and their stomachs become full. That stops the animals from eating food. They may then starve and die.

Coral Reef Killer

Plastic garbage in oceans is also affecting precious ecosystems. For example, when plastic waste lands on **coral reefs**, it blocks sunlight and the gas oxygen. Coral reefs need sunlight and oxygen to survive. Plastic also carries harmful **bacteria** to the reef. If coral comes into contact with the bacteria, it can become diseased. Coral reefs support thousands of animals. They include sharks and other fish, seahorses, and turtles. If coral reefs die, so do all the **organisms** that live on them.

Plastic packaging is often thrown away on beaches. It is also blown off boats at sea. It then makes its way into the ocean and onto coral reefs.

TAKING ECO ACTION:

A PLASTIC-FREE WORLD

The Plastic Pollution Coalition (PPC) is taking action against plastic. The PPC is a worldwide network of more than 1,200 organizations, businesses, and individuals who are committed to making the world free of plastic pollution. The network includes people from 75 countries. It educates people about the dangers of plastic. It shows them how they can live a plastic-free life.

Plastic-Free Lessons

The PPC has set up the Plastic Free Schools program. Its aim is to reduce plastic pollution in schools around the world. Involved schools and students are encouraged to carry out fund-raising and awareness-raising events. They include plastic-free sporting events. They also include campaigns to end the sale of bottled water in schools.

The program focuses on getting rid of food-related plastic items in schools.

PLASTIC-FREE CONNECTIONS

The PPC puts town communities in touch with other groups committed to dealing with the big issue of plastic in our oceans. These groups include the Clean Seas Coalition (CSC). This is a network of **environmentalists**, scientists, and lawmakers. It also includes students and community leaders. All members are committed to reducing and removing plastics from our beaches and our oceans.

Plastic-Free Eating Out

The PPC works with restaurants, cafés, and other places in which people eat out to change their use of plastic. It encourages organizations to:

- buy food in as little plastic packaging as possible
- use real plates, cutlery, and glasses instead of plastic ones
- use stainless steel food storage rather than plastic food storage
- provide glass or stainless steel drink **dispensers** instead of drinks in plastic bottles
- end the use of plastic straws, stir sticks, and plastic lids for cups
- use waxed paper or parchment to wrap food rather than plastic wrap
- carry out on-site food composting and recycling

Plastic-Free Towns

The PPC also works with towns to help them get rid of plastics. It works with local town organizations, from cafés to stores. It encourages them to reduce the amount of plastic food packaging and utensils they use. It also helps towns focus on the big problem of plastic shopping bags. The PPC encourages towns to get rid of plastic bags entirely.

Removing plastic waste from beaches is an important job. It reduces the amount of plastic that enters our oceans.

TAKE ECO ACTION AGAINST PACKAGING

Organizations like the PPC are taking positive action against plastic. And there are positive actions that you can take to cut back on harmful food packaging, too. By taking these eco actions, you'll be helping the planet and the animals that live on it.

Do You Really Need It?

Before you buy any foods, think about what you are buying. You can reduce waste by buying only the things you really need.

Ditch the Plastic

Avoid buying plastic-wrapped foods. Try to buy as much unpackaged food as you can. For example, buy unpackaged fruits and vegetables instead of those wrapped in plastic.

Ditch the Plastic Bags

Don't shop with plastic bags. Try to use mesh bags or fabric bags. They are made from sustainable materials and will rot when you eventually need to throw them away.

Choose Eco-Friendly

Try to buy food from eco-friendly stores. There, the packaging will have been carefully chosen so it does not harm the environment.

Just Say No!

If you are offered a plastic straw for your drink when you buy one, just say no! Drink the old-fashioned way, by sipping your drink from a glass. You can also take your own reusable straw with you when you go out. Say no to plastic drink lids, too.

Check Out the Packaging

Don't buy food packaged in mixed-material packaging that cannot easily be recycled. Buy foods packaged in just one material. For example, choose glass bottles rather than cartons made of plastic and cardboard.

Recycle It!

Carefully recycle any food packaging that you do buy. Try to separate materials so they are ready to be recycled. For example, separate the cardboard and plastic in food packaging. That will make the recycling process efficient.

Eco Action Wins

By cutting down on your food packaging, you'll be cutting down on landfill waste. You will also help tackle climate change. By reducing the amount of plastic packaging you buy, you'll be reducing the amount of plastic in our oceans. They are all eco wins for planet Earth!

CHAPTER 3

A GROWING PROBLEM

Not only is food waste and packaging a problem, so is the way we farm our food. The methods used to grow most crops are not sustainable. Neither is the way that livestock, or farm animals, are kept. Our farming practices are harming Earth, and it's time they changed.

A Meaty Problem

A lot of people in western countries, such as the United States, Canada, the United Kingdom, and Germany, eat a lot of meat. It is estimated that the average American eats about 264 pounds (120 kg) of meat a year. That's a lot of meat! The problem with eating so much meat is that it is not good for the planet. That's because farming meat uses more land and resources than any other type of food.

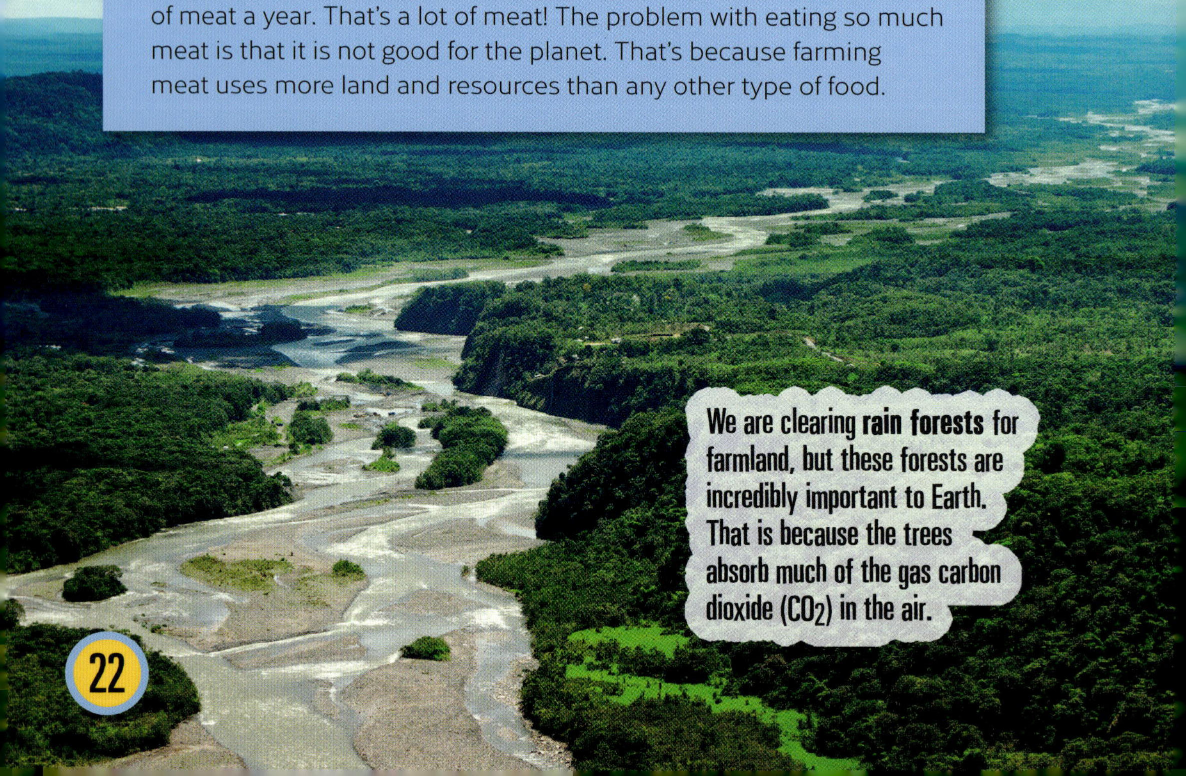

We are clearing **rain forests** for farmland, but these forests are incredibly important to Earth. That is because the trees absorb much of the gas carbon dioxide (CO_2) in the air.

Methane is far more damaging to the environment than carbon dioxide. By feeding our appetite for meat, we are feeding the atmosphere with this harmful gas.

Cut Down for Cattle

To feed our demand for meat, large areas of natural forest are being cleared for farming. And much of the livestock that is then kept on that land is cattle. Every year, around 6.7 million acres (2.7 million ha) of **tropical forest** is cleared so that cattle can be kept on it. In some areas of the Amazon Rain Forest, 70 percent of the plants and trees have been cut down to make room for cattle or the crops grown to feed them. The crops are often soybeans.

A Gas Planet

Not only does cutting down rain forest to make room for cattle add to our climate change problems, so do the cattle themselves. We have learned what a problem methane gas is. It is damaging if it is released into the atmosphere. The problem with cattle is that they release methane almost all of the time—as belches and farts! And when you add up how many cattle are now on Earth, you can see the scale of the methane problem. There are almost 1 billion cattle in the world today. That is a big, gassy problem for our planet.

EYE-WATERING WATER

Using up precious resources to make our food is a real issue. Did you know that about 80 percent of all the water used in the United States is used in farming? That's a lot of water! You might think that all of that water is used just to grow crops, but that isn't the case. In fact, farming cattle uses far more water than farming crops. It takes around 1,800 gallons (6,814 l) of water to produce just 1 pound (0.5 kg) of beef. To produce enough grain to make a loaf of bread, a farmer uses just 240 gallons (909 l) of water.

A FISHY PROBLEM

Our farming methods on land have had a huge impact on our planet. So have our food-sourcing methods at sea. A huge number of people around the world rely on fish for food. Fish is a great food source. It is high in protein. Protein is an important nutrient that helps us build muscle. Oily fish also supplies us with essential omega-3 fats. We need these fats to be healthy. Fish is good for us. But unfortunately, we have taken too many of some types of fish from our oceans.

Catching Cod

Just as we have farmed the land **intensively** to feed the growing human **population**, we have intensively fished the oceans for food. As the world's population has grown, so too has its demand for fish. One of the biggest fishing issues has been the catching of cod.

Cod is a large fish that is famous for its delicious white flesh. The fish is found in both the Atlantic and Pacific Oceans. Cod used to be widely found in the Atlantic Ocean. However, huge amounts of cod were fished in the Atlantic Ocean between the 1950s and the 1990s. The cod was caught very quickly and in huge numbers. As a result of this intensive fishing, too few young fish were left to replace the adult fish that had been caught. The remaining young fish couldn't reproduce, or have babies, quickly enough to replace the adult fish that had been caught. That meant the cod population could not replenish itself. That put the Atlantic Cod under threat.

Huge amounts of cod have been caught in the waters around the United Kingdom. There, the cod population has been badly damaged. It has not recovered from overfishing.

COMPLETELY CAUGHT OUT

Enormous amounts of cod fishing took place in one particular area of the Atlantic Ocean–the Grand Banks. This once cod-rich area is found off the northeastern coast of the United States and southeast of Newfoundland, Canada. Too much cod was caught around the Grand Banks. By 1992, the fish had nearly disappeared from the area. That led to the collapse of the fishing industries that relied on the fish.

Adult Pacific bluefin tuna can grow to a length of 4.9 feet (1.5 m) and weigh up to 130 pounds (59 kg).

A Hunger for Tuna

Overfishing has been a problem in other oceans, too. The Pacific Ocean is the biggest ocean on Earth. It supports many of the world's fishing industries. But, this ocean has been overfished, too. The Pacific bluefin tuna is one fish that has been caught in too great numbers. It was once fished to the point of extinction. Fishing laws now protect the tuna and have helped it recover. However, it is still considered to be an over-fished **species**.

TOO INTENSE

When topsoil is plowed by farm vehicles, the soil is disrupted and some of it may blow away in the wind.

Modern farming is often called intensive farming. That is because it involves getting as much food from an area of land as possible. Intensive farming helps us get more food. However, it does not help the planet. Up to one-third of Earth's soil has lost its nutrients due to overuse. When crops are grown, they absorb nutrients from the soil. If crops are continually grown on land, without rest between farming cycles, the soil loses its nutrients. Crops that are then grown on that soil contain fewer nutrients, too. That means when we eat those crops, our food is not as nourishing, or as good for us, as it should be.

Disappearing Soil

The world grows 95 percent of its food in Earth's uppermost layer of soil. It is called topsoil. However, because of intensive farming, almost half of the world's topsoil has disappeared in the last 150 years. Soil erosion is the removal of topsoil from an area of land. Soil erosion is caused by natural occurrences. Those include wind blowing away soil or water washing it away. But soil erosion is also caused by farming activities, such as turning over the soil to plant seeds in it. Soil is also removed when crops are harvested, or cut down for food. If we keep using our current farming methods, Earth's remaining topsoil could disappear within the next 60 years.

FEEDING THE WORLD

One of the reasons why intensive farming has taken place is that the world's population has been growing every year. In 1900, there were 1.6 billion people on Earth. In 2000, there were 6 billion people on the planet. By the year 2050, there may be as many as 9.6 billion people living on Earth! And all those people will need to be fed. We need to make sure that we protect our soil. We need to use smarter farming methods so that future populations will have enough food.

It is estimated that the population of Asia will reach 4.7 billion by the year 2100.

CHEMICAL CROPS

Intensive farming also involves using chemicals, such as fertilizers. Chemical fertilizers provide the plants with more nutrients, such as phosphorus and potassium. That helps the crops grow bigger and faster. They increase the amount of crops grown, too. However, chemicals in crop farming can cause many problems.

A Lesson in Chemistry

Chemical fertilizers can upset the natural balance of nutrients in the soil. They can make it too rich in some nutrients. That causes other important nutrients to be reduced or lost. When chemical fertilizers are added to soil, they can also be carried from the soil and into waterways when it rains. Important water habitats such as streams, rivers, lakes, and oceans can be damaged by the chemicals. So can land habitats. Plants and animals in those habitats may then be harmed by the chemicals, too.

These fish have died because their habitat was **contaminated** by artificial chemicals.

CHEMICALS AND CLIMATE CHANGE

The use of chemical fertilizers also adds to the problem of climate change. Chemical fertilizers are broken down in the soil by tiny organisms, called microbes. During this process, a greenhouse gas called nitrous oxide is released into the atmosphere. That adds to the blanket of greenhouse gases surrounding Earth, and increases **global warming**.

A Pesty Problem

Plants may be sprayed with insecticides. They are chemicals that kill insect pests that eat valuable crops. However, pesticides are a problem. Organisms other than crop pests live on or near the crops. When pesticides are sprayed onto farmland crops, those organisms may be killed along with the pests. The pesticides can also be washed away by rain. They are washed into waterways that flow through important habitats. The animals and plants that live there may then be harmed by the chemicals.

Harming Humans

Chemicals used in farming can also harm people. Some chemicals sprayed onto farm crops are known to have caused human health problems. The chemicals include the insecticide dichlorodiphenyltrichloroethane (DDT). It has been linked to many health issues. They include brain development problems in babies. They also include reproduction issues in adults. The use of DDT is now banned in many developed countries, including the United States.

DDT is still used in some developing countries. Here, it is being used in Thailand in Asia.

TAKING ECO ACTION:

GOING ORGANIC

Today, many farmers and food-producing organizations are turning to organic farming. That is a means of farming sustainably. Organic farming is a system in which high-quality food is created using methods that do not harm the environment or human health. The Florida Certified Organic Growers and Consumers Inc (FOG) is one organization that is taking eco action against intensive farming. The organization began in 1987. Its aim is to educate people about the benefits of organic food. Those people include food producers, food buyers, and people in government.

Organic farmers allow wild areas on their farmland. In them, crop-friendly insects and animals can make homes.

BUZZING WITH BIODIVERSITY

By encouraging wildlife onto farmland, organic farmers make their land biodiverse. A biodiverse environment includes many different types of plants and animals. Biodiversity is good for the planet.

Working with Farmers

FOG works with food producers to help them understand the best practices in organic farming. It gives producers the tools and information they need to farm sustainably. Part of FOG's education program is to show farmers that they can grow food without the use of chemical fertilizers and pesticides.

Organic farmers do not use chemical weed killers. They use pesticides only if absolutely necessary, and these are natural pesticides. They include oils such as citronella and clove. Rather than rely on pesticides, organic farmers try to create a healthy local wildlife population to control insect pests. They encourage creatures such as birds, beetles, and ladybugs onto their farms by creating habitats for them. In turn, these creatures eat crop-eating pests. They include aphids, slugs, and caterpillars. The pests are controlled naturally, without using chemical pesticides that harm the environment.

Caring for the Soil

FOG also explains how to grow food without the use ofchemical fertilizers. In organic farming, natural fertilizers such as animal **manure** are used. Organic farmers also rotate crops. That means that from one crop-growing season to another, they grow different crops on an area of land. They also allow areas of land to rest between crop-growing seasons. That is called fallowing. It helps the soil recover from crop growing. It helps the soil replenish its nutrients.

Helping Consumers

FOG also helps consumers make good food choices. It educates the public about organic food. It explains the health benefits of organic farming, and the benefits it provides to the planet. FOG connects consumers with local organic food suppliers. It also shows people how to grow and cook their own organic produce.

FOG connects people with organic food markets, at which they can buy food produced by organic farmers.

TAKE ECO ACTION AGAINST INTENSIVE FARMING

Organizations like FOG are taking positive action against intensive farming. And there are positive actions that you can take to encourage sustainable food production, too. By taking these eco actions, you'll be helping organic farmers. You'll also be helping the planet.

Support Local Farmers

Many organic farms have stores. In them, you can buy fruits, vegetables, and animal products. Ask your parents or guardians to find out where your local organic farm shops are and put them on your shopping list.

Buy Organic

Try to buy organic food as much as you can. That food will not have been grown with the use of harmful pesticides. Many grocery stores now stock organic fruits and vegetables. You can also find organic pasta, rice, and other grains.

Grow Your Own

Try growing your own fruits and vegetables. That way, you can make sure that you use only organic fertilizer, such as manure, to grow plants. If you grow your own fruits and vegetables, protect them from pests by using natural methods. For example, cover your plants with netting to keep away insects and birds.

Think About Meat

Try to buy meat only from farmers who raise their livestock sustainably. That is better for animals and the land. The meat is also better for you. Why not also ask your parents or guardians if you can make mealtimes meat-free on Mondays? By cutting down on just one meat meal a week, you'll be helping the planet.

Go Wild!

Make part of your garden biodiverse. Allow a section to be wild, so that a lot of different plants can grow there. It will become a mini wildlife zone, full of different organisms.

Be Fussy About Fish

Choose your fish carefully. Avoid buying fish, such as cod, that are threatened by overfishing.

Eco Action Wins

By choosing to buy organic food whenever you can, you will be supporting organic farmers. The more people buy organic food, the more farmers will create it. By checking carefully where your meat comes from, and choosing fish carefully, too, you can ensure it is sustainably sourced. By making part of your garden wild, you'll be helping to keep Earth biodiverse. They are all great eco wins for planet Earth!

ECO ACTION!

CHAPTER 4

FOOD ON THE GO

Have you ever thought about where your food comes from? Do you know if it is locally grown or farmed? Does it come from far away? Well, where our food comes from and how we get it to our plates has created a truckload of problems for our planet.

Pumping out Pollution

Today, we readily transport food across the world. Our food can cover huge distances before it reaches our plates. We have come to expect fresh tropical fruits whenever we want them—even if it is winter where we are living! Many people love to eat avocados. However, these delicious fruits often must be transported from faraway places. Foods such as these might be transported by truck, ship, and plane to reach the places where they are sold. All those vehicles are powered by fossil fuels, such as gasoline. As they transport food, they release harmful carbon dioxide into Earth's atmosphere. That contributes to global warming and climate change.

Many of the avocados we eat grow on trees in South America.

MILES AND MILES OF FOOD

Have you heard of the term "food miles?" This refers to the number of miles a food has traveled from where it was sourced to where it is sold. For example, if you buy a banana at your local store, it has accumulated food miles. The banana will have racked up food miles in its journey from the tree it grew to the store in which it is sold. Food miles are a problem because for every mile traveled by a food, pollution will have been pumped into the atmosphere by the vehicle transporting that food.

It is estimated that, on average, most meals eaten in the United States have traveled around 1,491 miles (2,400 km) in food miles! Those miles may have been traveled by plane, ship, truck, and train.

Future Food Droughts

We are even making it more difficult to produce food in some parts of the world because we are transporting it so widely. Climate change is causing some parts of the world to have droughts. During a drought, crops fail. They cannot grow without water. Droughts also turn areas of land that were once **fertile** into deserts where nothing can grow. By pumping out greenhouse gases through food transportation, we are destroying land we desperately need for farming food.

FOOD THAT ISN'T FAIR

When we buy food that has been grown far away overseas, we don't always buy it fairly. Producers in developing areas, such as parts of Africa and Asia, are often not paid a reasonable price for the food they sell. Large companies in countries such as the United States, Canada, and Europe may buy the food cheaply. They then sell it in those countries for a lot more money. They do so to make a **profit**. That is not fair to the food producers, and it is not sustainable.

Many children in developing parts of the world work on farmland.

Cheap Crops Quickly

There are 736 million people around the world who live in extreme poverty. Of that number, 80 percent live in **rural** areas. Those people rely on farming to earn a living. But, they are not paid a fair price for the food they produce.

To produce food to sell at cheap prices, farmers in developing countries must produce that food cheaply. That means they must use chemical fertilizers to make crops grow quickly. It means they must clear natural habitats to make more space for crops. That destroys local habitats and ecosystems, and further harms our planet.

Working Hard, Earning Little

Having to produce food cheaply and sell it at unfairly low prices also harms the people who help produce it. Many people in developing countries are employed in food production. They are often paid incredibly low wages to work. Some are paid nothing—they are forced to work for free. Even children are made to work. Around the world, 152 million children work as child laborers. Of that number, 70 percent work in agriculture. Much of the foods that we enjoy every day are produced because of the use of unfair child and adult labor in countries far away. That is anything but a fair deal.

These women are harvesting tea leaves in India. Some other foods we buy from overseas countries include coffee, sugar, cocoa, and rice.

NOT-SO-SWEET CHOCOLATE

In West Africa, a lot of cocoa is produced. It is bought by food companies in western countries, so that people there can enjoy chocolate foods and drinks. However, the cocoa is bought at a cheap price. To produce enough cocoa to make a living, farmers have cut down large areas of forest in West Africa to make room for cocoa crops. This large-scale cutting down of forest is called deforestation. It destroys animal habitats. It wipes out plants that grow in the forest, too. That reduces biodiversity and damages ecosystems. It is not sustainable farming.

TAKING ECO ACTION:

A FREE TRADE

More and more Fairtrade food products are now being sold around the world. They include tea, coffee, sugar, and chocolate.

Fairtrade is an organization that is taking action against unfair food prices and unsustainable farming. Fairtrade is made up of a network of farmers in developing areas. It includes 25 organizations that **promote** and sell the food that the farmers produce. Also part of the network are inspectors. These people visit farms to ensure food produced on them is created sustainably.

How Does Fairtrade Work?

The 25 organizations that represent farmers in the Fairtrade network promote their products to food buyers in developed countries. The food is sold at a fair price, and the farmers receive that money.

Fairtrade represents farmers in Africa, the Middle East, and Asia. It also represents farmers in the Pacific area, Latin America, and the Caribbean.

Better for People

By earning a fair price for their produce, Fairtrade farmers can afford to use sustainable farming methods. They include organic farming practices. They also include properly paid labor and not using slave or child labor. The farmers themselves earn a better wage. That means their quality of life is improved. They can afford better housing. They can afford to send their children to school. That means in the future, those children will have a better chance of earning a good living themselves.

Better for the Planet

Fairtrade benefits the environment. By paying farmers a fair price for food, they do not have to produce as much of it. That means they do not have to cut down so much natural habitat to make room for farm crops. As a result, wildlife in those habitats can live safely there. Plants that live in those habitats thrive. Entire ecosystems are protected.

When people are paid properly for their work, they are more likely to follow sustainable farming practices.

A PRICE WORTH PAYING

Fairtrade products might cost more than non-Fairtrade products. However, people who buy them know that they are helping farmers earn a fair price for their crops. They are also helping the environment. It's a fair price to pay for those benefits.

TAKE ECO ACTION AGAINST UNSUSTAINABLE FARMING

Organizations like Fairtrade are taking positive action against unsustainable farming and unfair trade. And there are positive actions that you can take to encourage sustainable farming around the world, too. By taking these eco actions, you'll be helping farmers and their families. You'll be helping the people who work for them. And you'll be helping the planet.

Make Sure It's a Fair Trade

Ask your parents or guardians to try to buy Fairtrade products. Ask them to look carefully for the Fairtrade label on goods such as tea, coffee, chocolate, and sugar. Tell everyone that it's worth paying a little extra to make sure that food is fairly produced and bought. There are 12,000 Fairtrade products available in the United States. Make sure you buy some of them!

Cut Your Food Miles

Research the foods that you eat. Are they locally grown, or have they traveled from far overseas before they reach your plate? Think about how many food miles your family clocks up every week. Discuss with your parents or guardians how you could cut down on food miles. You can find out more about food miles and how they are calculated on page 47 of this book.

Follow the Seasons

Try to eat foods that are in season where you live. In season means that produce grows naturally where you live in the season you buy it. The best and easiest way to do this is to check out the Seasonal Food Guide. This awesome guide will show you exactly what produce is available year-around wherever you live. You can find the website address for this resource on page 47. You can also grow your own fruits and vegetables. That way, it's easy to follow the seasons.

Keep It Local

If you buy foods from local farm shops, it's easy to buy foods that are in season. And if you eat out, try to find restaurants or cafés that serve in-season foods, too. Many eateries now feature in-season foods on their menus as part of their plan to help protect the planet.

Eco Action Wins

By choosing to buy Fairtrade foods, you'll be supporting farmers around the world who need a fair price for their goods. It will mean they will have enough money to carry out sustainable farming. That will protect natural habitats, such as rain forests. By checking out your food miles, you can think about how you can reduce them. If you eat in-season foods, that will also cut down on food transportation. It will support local producers, too. Those are all great eco wins for planet Earth and its people!

ECO ACTION!

CONCLUSION

AN EARTH-FRIENDLY FOOD FUTURE

There are many challenges facing our food future, including the challenge of sustainably feeding a growing population. Thankfully, smart new technologies are helping us rise to that challenge. And we have only to look to the Netherlands to see how best to use them.

Neat Ideas from the Netherlands

The Netherlands has become one of the biggest food **exporters** in the world. And it is exporting sustainably produced foods. Yet, this country is 270 times smaller than the United States! So how has this little country produced so much food?

Many food production companies in the Netherlands are using smart technology to create fruits and vegetables. For example, one tomato producer called Duijvestijn Tomaten has created very tall glasshouses. In them, large numbers of tomato plants are grown in tall vertical lines.

Duijvestijn Tomaten grows 100 million tomatoes a year on just 34.5 acres (14 ha) of land! That is a fraction of the land space that would be required in traditional farming. Other fruit and vegetable producers are now following their lead.

If we could create cultured meat on a worldwide scale, it really could be one of the biggest eco food wins of all time!

The glasshouse has a double-glass roof. The roof helps the glasshouse hold on to heat. It is also fitted with LED lights, which stay on all night to help the plants grow. The CO_2 that feeds the tomato plants is captured from a local **oil refinery**. It is then pumped into the glasshouses. That stops the CO_2 escaping from the refinery into the atmosphere. It also provides the plants with the gas they need to grow. That's a big eco win!

Earth-Friendly Meat

Smart solutions to our demand for meat are also being found—in science labs. Scientists have created a method of "growing" meat such as beef by using **cells** from live cattle. The cells are kept in test tubes, in which they are fed nutrients. The cells then multiply, until they form a complete piece of meat, such as a piece of steak.

Some scientists argue that growing cultured meat is the most environmentally friendly way of making food that has ever been created. If enough cultured meat can be made available to people around the world, it means we would no longer need to keep livestock. That would mean no more cutting down of precious forests to make room for livestock. It would also mean no more production of methane from cattle. And it would mean that more and more hungry people around the world could be fed in the future.

A Brighter Food Future

Although there are challenges to be faced in our food-production future, we are facing them with better technology than ever before. We are also facing them with a new attitude of living sustainably. If we take eco action now, and invest in smart science and technology, we can all have a fair and Earth-friendly food future.

BUILD A CAREER IN ECO ACTION

Why not take more eco action, and develop a career in Earth-friendly foods? There are many different career paths that you can explore. And they will all help the planet move toward a sustainable food future. Imagine the difference your generation could make to Earth by making a career out of eco action. Here are just some of the areas that you could explore.

Get into Eco Farming

There are a huge number of different jobs available today in sustainable farming. Many colleges now offer a degree qualification in Sustainable Agriculture and Food Systems (SAFS). Qualified students can go on to carve out a career in lots of different fields. These include being a sustainable farmer, training farmers in sustainability, and researching sustainable food production as a technician in a lab. Studying subjects at school such as science and math could help pave the way for a future in this area.

Get into Eco Stores and Eateries

If you think you would enjoy working with the general public, working in or running an eco-friendly food store could be a great choice for you. You would work directly with food suppliers to buy and stock their goods. You would educate the public about the best food choices for them. Why not also explore working for local food markets or eco cafés? If you choose a career in these areas, having a business qualification would be useful. A qualification in food nutrition may also be useful. Studying subjects at school such as business, math, science, and food science could help you develop your future.

Educating people about earth-friendly food choices is a great way to build an eco action career.

Get into Eco Food Trade

By working for an organization such as Fairtrade, you could make a real difference to farmers and families in developing countries. Fairtrade and similar organizations have many roles, from fundraising in an office through to working directly with farmers in countries around the world. Studying subjects at school such as geography, science, business, languages, and math could help you in the future.

Get into Ocean Protection

Why not take up the fight against plastic pollution in our oceans? By becoming a **marine biologist**, you will get to monitor what effect plastic is having on oceans and ocean wildlife. Armed with that information, you will be able to inform people in government and organizations about what is happening to our oceans. You will be able to work with conservation groups to help clean up our shores and oceans, and protect them for the future. Useful subjects to study at school are science and geography.

By becoming a marine biologist, you will study ocean life and the effects human action is having on it.

Get into Sustainable Packaging

By helping create more sustainable food packaging, you could help reduce and end the problem of landfills and plastic pollution on Earth. Food manufacturing and packaging companies rely on scientists and **technologists** to develop more sustainable packaging. Studying subjects at school such as science, math, and design and technology will help you in this field.

GLOSSARY

atmosphere the layer of gases that surrounds Earth
bacteria very simple living organisms
cells the smallest parts of living things
climate the regular weather conditions of an area
contaminated made dirty or polluted
coral reefs structures found on the seabed in warm waters, made up of the skeletons of tiny organisms
dispensers devices that give out something, such as drinks
droughts periods of time with little or no rain
ecosystem a system made up of plants and animals and the things they need to survive, such as air, sunlight, and water
environment a natural place that surrounds plants and animals
environmentalists people who want to protect environments
exporters people or organizations that sell their products to buyers overseas
fertile able to produce
floods the movement of large amounts of water over land that is normally dry
food poverty having little or no food
fossil fuels fuels such as coal, oil, and gas that were made from animals and plants that died long ago
global warming an increase in Earth's temperatures, caused by human actions
habitat a natural place in which plants and animals live
hurricanes powerful storms with heavy rain and strong winds
intensively producing a lot in a relatively small space
manufacturers people or organizations that make things
manure animal waste
marine biologist a scientist who studies ocean life
minerals substances in food that help maintain a healthy body
oil refinery a place in which oil found in its natural state is turned into fuel such as gasoline
organisms living things, such as plants and animals
pandemic a disease that affects a number of parts of the world
pollution harmful substances in the air, land, or water
population the number of people or living organisms in one place
profit money left after costs are paid
promote to support or advertise a product or service to possible buyers
rain forests areas with many trees that experience regular heavy rainfall
recycling turning waste into something that can be used again
redistributing taking something from one place and giving it out to a different group of people or in a different way
resource a material or supply that can be used to make or produce something
reusable can be used again
rural away from towns and cities
species a group of similar living things that can mate with one another
technologists people who are skilled in the theory and practice of a technical profession
tropical forest a forest found near the equator
wildfires large fires that spread quickly through natural areas

FIND OUT MORE

Books

Hamby, Rachel. *Saving the Oceans from Plastic* (Saving Earth's Biomes). Mendota Heights, MN: North Star Editions, 2021.

Rebman, Nick. *Earth-Friendly Transportation* (Helping the Environment). Mendota Heights, MN: North Star Editions, 2021.

Woodward, John. *Climate Change* (DK Eyewitness). London, UK: DK Children, 2021.

Websites

Calculate your food miles at:
www.bbc.com/future/bespoke/follow-the-food/calculate-the-environmental-footprint-of-your-food.html

Discover what one organic farm is doing to help Earth at:
www.earthboundfarm.com

Find out lots more about careers in conservation at:
www.environmentalscience.org/careers

Discover more about Fairtrade products and how the organization is helping people and the planet at:
www.fairtradecertified.org

Learn more about Feeding America and how you can help take action against food poverty at:
www.feedingamerica.org/take-action

Find out how you can eat in-season foods with the Seasonal Food Guide:
www.seasonalfoodguide.org

INDEX

About the Author

Sarah Eason has written many books for children on a wide variety of topics, including history, science, and geography. In researching this book, she has discovered how important it is that we all take eco action to protect our planet—starting right now!